AI AND KEEPING YOUR JOB

The Glacier series on asking AI

David Glacier

DAVID GLACIER
PUBLISHING

Dedicated to Colleen

"AI will not replace humans but those who use AI will replace those who don't."

GINNI ROMETTY, FORMER CEO OF IBM

CONTENTS

Title Page

Copyright

Dedication

Epigraph

How is AI reshaping the very definition of work?   2

Will AI make work more about creativity and problem-solving   4
than routine tasks?

Could AI eliminate work as we know it, or will it simply   6
transform it?

How will AI impact the meaning people derive from their   8
jobs?

Which industries will AI disrupt most profoundly?   10

What new kinds of jobs might AI create that don't exist   12
today?

How can workers prepare for careers in an AI-driven   14
economy?

Will AI accelerate the decline of certain professions, like law,   16
medicine, or teaching?

How can humans and AI collaborate most effectively in the   18
workplace?

What does it mean to have an AI co-worker?   20

Could AI improve workplace safety and reduce hazardous   22 labor?

How do we balance efficiency with the need for human 25
oversight?

Will AI widen the gap between high-skilled and low-skilled 27
workers?

Could AI reduce global inequality by providing access to 29
tools and knowledge

What role might universal basic income play in an AI- 31
transformed economy?

How do we prevent concentration of AI power in the hands 33
of a few corporations?

How will AI affect the sense of identity people derive from 36
their work?

Could widespread automation lead to a crisis of purpose for 38
many individuals?

Might AI allow people to pursue projects of passion instead 40
of traditional jobs?

How do we redefine success in a world where AI handles 42
much of the labor?

Could AI make the 4-day workweek or even the end of the 44
workweek possible?

How will AI influence the future of unions and worker 47
rights?

What role will AI play in global supply chains and the 49
concept of 'essential'

Could AI manage entire organizations or governments 52
without human oversight?

Ultimately, will AI liberate humanity from work or tether us 54
more tightly to new forms of labor?

Conclusion 56

Notes 68

72

74

76

78

80

Introduction

In the shadow of every technological revolution stands a single question: *What becomes of human work?* With the rise of artificial intelligence, this question takes on sharper edges, deeper implications and more uncertain answers. For the first time in history, machines are not just performing tasks they are thinking, learning and adapting. That shift doesn't merely change what we do. It changes how we define ourselves.

This book does not aim to predict the future in exact terms, no machine or mind can. Instead, it invites reflection, speculation and conversation. Through a series of questions posed to AI and curated with care, we explore how intelligence, both artificial and human, intertwines in the evolving definition of work.

What follows is not prophecy but provocation. Each interview is a snapshot of possibility, a nudge toward understanding what might lie ahead. Whether you are hopeful, anxious, skeptical or curious, this book is for you because the future of work will not only be designed by engineers and economists but by all of us.

Preface

Because much of the content in this interview is AI-generated I'd like the reader to keep in mind that the questions posed in any AI conversation shape the answers you receive. The wording of a question can introduce bias. So can the order in which the questions are asked.

That's part of what makes working with AI both fascinating and fragile. Unlike a human, an AI doesn't forget what came before, not until the conversation ends. Each prompt builds on the last, sometimes subtly. You can steer it without realizing you're steering it. You can confirm your own assumptions without intending to.

That doesn't make AI useless. It makes it different.

This book doesn't try to simulate a live debate or a definitive point of view. It's closer to a series of reflections prompted by a human, shaped by a machine and edited with care. The questions come from me. The answers come from AI, though some have been tightened or trimmed for clarity.

This process introduces its own limitations. Once a session ends, you can't return to ask AI to revise earlier responses. You can't ask the AI to remember what it said ten pages ago from a previous conversation. There's no continuity in the way we're used to, therefore some overlap will appear in the AI's answers. Certain themes may resurface more than once.

But maybe that's fitting. Work itself is repetitive. As are the questions we ask about the future: *What happens to my job? What happens to my value?* And now, *What happens when AI enters the room?*

This book is one way of sitting with those questions without pretending the answers are simple or settled.

THE INTERVIEW

HOW IS AI RESHAPING THE VERY DEFINITION OF WORK?

When people talk about work today, it no longer sounds much like it did twenty, or even ten, years ago. For most of modern history, work meant physical presence, repetitive tasks and productivity measured in hours logged or units produced. Artificial intelligence is quietly rewriting that definition, nudging society toward a version of work that is less about time and place and more about creativity, problem-solving and adaptability. It is worth pausing on this shift, because it affects not only the kinds of jobs people hold but also how human contribution itself is valued.

AI is reshaping work by moving routine, repetitive tasks out of human hands. Data entry, document review, scheduling and even customer service inquiries once consumed hours of labor but are now increasingly automated. This shift not only saves resources but also changes what is considered real work. If machines handle the mechanical parts of a task, then what remains for humans often involves judgment, nuance and creativity. Instead of entering numbers into spreadsheets, employees may now interpret the patterns behind those numbers and advise on strategy. Work moves from execution to interpretation.

There is also a psychological dimension. For generations, people measured their worth at work by effort: how hard or how long they toiled. But when AI systems can churn through mountains of data in seconds, effort alone no longer defines value. Increasingly, value arises from insight, originality and human connection. This forces a subtle but profound rethinking: work is not only what provides a living but also what humans contribute that machines cannot. It reopens questions that are not often asked. Which parts of intelligence are uniquely human and how should societies cultivate them?

Another transformation lies in the dissolving boundaries between industries. AI does not respect the neat categories humans created. A doctor's work was once defined by diagnosis and treatment; now it includes partnering with AI systems that suggest possible conditions from patient scans. A medical student may rely on AI for study support. Lawyers use it to draft briefs or analyze precedent. Architects generate hundreds of design options in minutes with AI assistance. Professional identity is no longer bound to a narrow set of tasks. Instead, it becomes a blend of human oversight, machine collaboration and creative direction. This hybrid form of work challenges the very definition of expertise. Expertise is less about personal knowledge alone and more about guiding technology toward better outcomes.

These changes are not without tension. If AI assumes part of a role, does that make human work less valuable or more so? The answer depends on perspective. For some, automation threatens stability by undermining skills built over decades. For others, it represents liberation, freeing them from drudgery and opening space for higher-order work. The real challenge lies less in whether AI replaces jobs and more in how societies, companies and individuals respond—whether they re-skill, reimagine and adapt quickly enough to keep pace.

If work is seen primarily as human–AI collaboration, then qualities such as flexibility, curiosity and lifelong learning become paramount. Work evolves from a static identity into a fluid practice. In this sense, AI is not only changing what people do but also reshaping how society views the very meaning of work. The cultural shift may be uncomfortable but it holds promise: a future where work is less about rote labor and more about human ingenuity.

WILL AI MAKE WORK MORE ABOUT CREATIVITY AND PROBLEM-SOLVING THAN ROUTINE TASKS?

When people talk about work today, it no longer sounds much like it did twenty, or even ten, years ago. For most of modern history, work meant physical presence, repetitive tasks and productivity measured in hours logged or units produced. Artificial intelligence is quietly rewriting that definition, nudging society toward a version of work that is less about time and place and more about creativity, problem-solving and adaptability. It is worth pausing on this shift, because it affects not only the kinds of jobs people hold but also how human contribution itself is valued.

AI is reshaping work by moving routine, repetitive tasks out of human hands. Data entry, document review, scheduling and even customer service inquiries once consumed hours of labor but are now increasingly automated. This shift not only saves resources but also changes what is considered real work. If machines handle the mechanical parts of a task, then what remains for humans often involves judgment, nuance and creativity. Instead of entering numbers into spreadsheets, employees may now interpret the patterns behind those numbers and advise on strategy. Work moves from execution to interpretation.

There is also a psychological dimension. For generations, people measured their worth at work by effort: how hard or how long they toiled. But when AI systems can churn through mountains of data in seconds, effort alone no longer defines value. Increasingly, value arises from insight, originality and human connection. This forces a subtle but profound rethinking: work is not only what provides a living but also what humans contribute that machines cannot. It reopens questions that are not often asked. Which parts of intelligence are uniquely human and how should societies cultivate them?

Another transformation lies in the dissolving boundaries between industries. AI does not respect the neat categories humans created. A doctor's work was once defined by diagnosis and treatment; now it includes partnering with AI systems that suggest possible conditions from patient scans. A medical student may rely on AI for study support. Lawyers use it to draft briefs or analyze precedent. Architects generate hundreds of design options in minutes with AI assistance. Professional identity is no longer bound to a narrow set of tasks. Instead, it becomes a blend of human oversight, machine collaboration and creative direction. This hybrid form of work challenges the very definition of expertise. Expertise is less about personal knowledge alone and more about guiding technology toward better outcomes.

These changes are not without tension. If AI assumes part of a role, does that make human work less valuable or more so? The answer depends on perspective. For some, automation threatens stability by undermining skills built over decades. For others, it represents liberation, freeing them from drudgery and opening space for higher-order work. The real challenge lies less in whether AI replaces jobs and more in how societies, companies and individuals respond—whether they re-skill, reimagine and adapt quickly enough to keep pace.

If work is seen primarily as human–AI collaboration, then qualities such as flexibility, curiosity and lifelong learning become paramount. Work evolves from a static identity into a fluid practice. In this sense, AI is not only changing what people do but also reshaping how society views the very meaning of work. The cultural shift may be uncomfortable but it holds promise: a future where work is less about rote labor and more about human ingenuity.

COULD AI ELIMINATE WORK AS WE KNOW IT, OR WILL IT SIMPLY TRANSFORM IT?

When people ask whether AI could eliminate work, they are touching on one of the oldest anxieties in human history: the fear that a new machine will take away livelihoods. Every major technological shift has carried that question. The loom was expected to end weaving as a profession. The tractor was predicted to make farm labor obsolete. The computer was said to threaten millions of office jobs. In each case, some roles disappeared but work as a whole did not vanish—it changed shape. AI raises the stakes because it is not only automating muscle but also certain forms of brainpower. That makes the question sharper: is this the end of work as it has been known, or a transformation of what work means?

The truth lies in transformation. Work is deeply woven into human culture. It is not only a means of making a living but also a source of identity, community and purpose. Even if AI systems become capable of performing a vast range of tasks, societies will create new roles for humans—either to complement technology or to satisfy the enduring human need for contribution and recognition. People seek not only income but also meaning and that pursuit helps keep the structure of work alive in some form.

That transformation could, however, be radical. Imagine an economy where AI handles logistics, manufacturing, basic healthcare diagnostics, customer service and much of professional analysis. What remains for humans might not resemble the traditional nine-to-five. Labor could instead concentrate around oversight, creativity, emotional intelligence and fields not yet imagined. Just as the internet created jobs that would have seemed absurd in 1985—such as social media manager, app developer, or influencer—AI is likely to generate new categories of work that now seem unimaginable.

There is also a theoretical scenario in which AI becomes so advanced that it performs nearly all productive labor better and more cheaply than humans. If that were to occur, work in its current sense might be eliminated. The challenge then would not be technological but societal. Society would need to decide how to distribute wealth and resources in a world where human labor is no longer the backbone of the economy. Some thinkers see this as an opening for policies such as universal basic income or a redefinition of citizenship rights to include access to AI-generated abundance. Others warn that such a transition could be chaotic, deepening inequality between those who control the technology and those who do not.

More realistically, in the near to medium term AI will hollow out certain kinds of work while amplifying others. Routine jobs in accounting, transportation, or administration are particularly vulnerable. Roles requiring trust, empathy and complex interaction—such as teaching, caregiving, or leadership —are more resilient. This hollowing out and amplification would shift the concept of work into a spectrum of roles, redistributing emphasis rather than erasing the idea of work altogether.

Even if AI could take over most tasks, many people would resist surrendering the sense of agency and achievement that comes from working. Societies may choose to preserve certain forms of human labor not because machines cannot perform them but because humans value doing them. A world where art, sport, craftsmanship, or service are pursued out of choice rather than necessity might not resemble traditional work but would still embody meaningful human activity.

The question remains: will AI eliminate work? It is possible in the narrow sense of eliminating many current jobs. Yet history suggests a broader pattern—work transforms rather than disappears. Humans adapt, create new forms of labor and redefine what it means to contribute. AI may shake the foundations of work but it is more likely to transform its structure than to level it entirely.

HOW WILL AI IMPACT THE MEANING PEOPLE DERIVE FROM THEIR JOBS?

Work has never been only about earning money. For many people, a job provides purpose, structure and even part of their identity. This is why people often ask others, 'What do you do?' as a way of getting to know them. The challenge AI introduces is not merely about changing tasks or industries; it is about reshaping the meaning people attach to their work. That is a far more personal and sometimes unsettling, shift.

When AI begins to handle the routine and repetitive parts of a job, the result can feel liberating. A teacher freed from endless grading because an AI system evaluates multiple-choice tests, or a doctor who no longer spends hours completing paperwork because AI records and organizes patient notes, may both find greater fulfillment. In such cases, people are able to focus on the aspects of their professions that originally inspired them—connecting with students, guiding patients, or addressing big-picture challenges. In this sense, AI has the potential to deepen the human side of work by highlighting what feels most rewarding.

Yet the other side of the story is more complicated. For some, meaning comes from the mastery of a skill or the steady rhythm of tasks that AI now takes away. A craftsman may find satisfaction in the precision of repetitive labor. An accountant may take pride in balancing the books to the last cent. If AI performs these tasks faster and more accurately, an individual's sense of contribution and pride may erode. People may begin to wonder what role remains for them if machines can perform their work more effectively. This question is not only practical—it reaches the core of self-worth.

There is also the risk of disconnection. If AI absorbs too much of the challenge, human roles may shift toward mere oversight, where workers monitor system outputs rather than shape them. For some, that may feel like losing the heart of their work. Complacency may set in. It is one thing to be the decision-maker; it is another to feel like a passive observer in one's own profession.

In such cases, the meaning of work could diminish, driving individuals to seek fulfillment outside of their careers.

At the same time, AI could broaden what society considers meaningful work. If basic survival needs can be met with less human labor, more people may pursue roles chosen for passion rather than necessity. Art, caregiving, mentoring and community building—often undervalued in traditional economies—could gain new recognition. In a world reshaped by AI, meaning might shift away from being defined by production toward being defined by contribution to the human experience. This could redefine success in healthier, more human-centered ways.

Transitions of this scale are rarely smooth. Meaning is not only individually constructed; it is also shaped by culture and institutions. If businesses focus solely on efficiency and cost savings, they may overlook the importance of human fulfillment. By contrast, organizations that redesign work to promote ownership, creativity and responsibility could help employees find deeper satisfaction in an AI-driven world. Governments and communities, too, will play a role in guiding this shift, shaping policies and narratives that affirm human dignity without reducing it to competition with machines.

Ultimately, AI's impact on the meaning of work will depend on the choices societies and individuals make. AI could hollow out jobs, leaving people detached, or it could elevate them, allowing humans to engage more fully with the aspects of work that truly matter. Perhaps the greatest challenge of all is psychological: accepting that meaning need not come from being faster, stronger, or more precise than a machine. Instead, meaning can be found in connection, creativity and contribution—qualities that remain profoundly and perhaps uniquely, human.

WHICH INDUSTRIES WILL AI DISRUPT MOST PROFOUNDLY?

Some describe AI as a tidal wave about to sweep across the entire economy. In a sense, that is true. AI's reach will eventually extend to nearly every sector but the depth of disruption will not be uniform. Industries built on routine, data-heavy processes are already feeling the tremors, while those grounded in relationships, intuition, or creativity experience more resistance. This contrast reveals where the ground is shifting most profoundly.

Few industries generate more data than healthcare, from lab results to imaging scans to patient histories. AI is already proving itself a powerful diagnostic assistant, spotting patterns in X-rays or MRIs that even specialists might overlook. This does not make doctors irrelevant; rather, their role may become more human-focused. Healthcare overall will look different, with AI streamlining administration, assisting in drug discovery and potentially altering how patients interact with providers. Such disruption touches not only efficiency but also trust and care—two of the deepest foundations of medicine.

Finance is another sector being reshaped. Banks, insurance firms and investment companies thrive on data analysis and prediction, tasks AI can perform at superhuman speed. Algorithmic trading has long existed but today AI also assesses creditworthiness, detects fraud and provides personalized advice. For consumers, this promises faster, more tailored service. For workers, it may reduce roles in middle management or back-office analysis, while emphasizing client guidance where empathy and trust are essential.

Education, though less obvious, is on the edge of transformation. Personalized learning powered by AI tutors could adapt lessons to individual students in real time. Teachers may shift from content delivery to facilitating critical thinking and social development. This represents a deep change in how societies understand education and the value teachers bring. If managed well, the shift could make learning more inclusive and engaging; if mishandled, it risks reducing education to a sterile transfer of information.

Manufacturing and logistics, long influenced by automation, are also evolving under AI. Factories that once used rigidly programmed robots now employ adaptable machines capable of handling varied tasks. In logistics, AI optimizes supply chains, predicts delays and even powers autonomous trucks. These changes ripple outward, altering not only industries themselves but also the global flow of goods on which economies depend.

Even creative fields are not exempt. Media, marketing and entertainment now use AI to generate music, design logos, draft articles and write scripts. Some view this as a threat to human creativity, while others see it as an expanded toolkit. The disruption lies less in replacing humans and more in challenging notions of originality and ownership in the creative process.

What ties all these industries together is their reliance on information—how it is processed, applied and used to shape decisions. AI, at its core, is an engine for pattern recognition and prediction. Sectors most dependent on those functions will feel the strongest shockwaves. Yet disruption does not necessarily mean destruction. In many cases, AI may act as an accelerant, amplifying human capabilities rather than erasing them.

The real test is how industries choose to integrate these tools. Those that treat AI as a partner rather than a threat may not only endure disruption but thrive because of it. Ultimately, the most profound disruption may not be within any one sector but in how society conceives the relationship between human skill and machine intelligence.

WHAT NEW KINDS OF JOBS MIGHT AI CREATE THAT DON'T EXIST TODAY?

One of the most intriguing questions is not which jobs AI will replace but which it will create. Every major technological leap has generated new forms of work. Electricity produced roles like electrical engineers and appliance designers. The internet gave rise to web developers, social media managers and digital marketers—jobs unimaginable in the 1970s. AI will be no different. As its capabilities expand, it will spark new fields that today are only faintly visible.

Some of these roles are already taking shape. AI trainers and explainability specialists, for instance, refine how models learn and translate their reasoning into terms humans can trust. Entire careers may emerge around ensuring AI systems are transparent, ethical and aligned with human values—tasks requiring human judgment, empathy and communication.

Other roles will focus on maintaining and guiding AI systems as they inevitably stumble. Just as software engineers safeguard digital infrastructure today, future AI maintenance experts may diagnose when models drift into error, bias, or misuse. Protecting AI from manipulation or exploitation could itself become a major industry, much like cybersecurity is now.

Still other possibilities emerge at the intersection of AI and creativity. Synthetic experience designers could craft immersive, AI-driven environments for entertainment, therapy, or education. Instead of designing traditional games, they might build adaptive worlds that respond to participants' emotions in real time. Similarly, AI-assisted healthcare companions could combine professional expertise with AI tools to provide personalized coaching for fitness, mental health, or chronic illness management.

Another likely area is data stewardship. As AI depends on vast amounts of information, new professions may arise around helping individuals control, monetize and protect their digital footprints. Such roles could become guardians of human autonomy in a world where data is as valuable as oil once was.

Not all of these future jobs will sound technical. As AI takes over routine tasks, societies may place greater value on roles highlighting distinctly human qualities. Counselors may use AI to detect subtle emotional cues, while artists may collaborate with AI to expand creative horizons. These hybrid professions will rely on both human imagination and machine power.

The jobs AI creates will likely emerge where human needs and machine capabilities intersect. They will not be confined to engineers but will include hybrid positions blending human insight with machine intelligence. Just as nobody foresaw the rise of app developers when the first cell phones appeared, society may not yet have the vocabulary for many of the career's AI will unlock.

Rather than viewing AI as the end of jobs, it may be more accurate to see it as the beginning of a new chapter in work. The future will almost certainly surprise but history suggests that human ingenuity meets technological change not with extinction but with reinvention.

HOW CAN WORKERS PREPARE FOR
CAREERS IN AN AI-DRIVEN ECONOMY?

Preparing for a career in an AI-driven economy is not about memorizing coding languages or racing to outpace machines; it is about developing qualities and skills that will remain valuable no matter how technology evolves. History suggests that the future belongs to those who adapt. When industrial machines transformed manual labor, workers learned new trades. When computers arrived in offices, employees developed digital literacy. AI is simply the next chapter in that story, though it demands broader readiness and greater mental flexibility. Success will depend on continuous learning and a willingness to work alongside intelligent systems rather than against them.

One of the most important shifts is moving away from thinking of careers as static. For much of the twentieth century, people trained in one field and often remained there for decades. That stability is now less common. In an AI-driven world, careers will be more fluid, requiring reinvention multiple times over. Workers who treat learning as a lifelong habit—taking courses, experimenting with new tools and staying curious about emerging trends—will gain an edge. The most resilient employees will not be those who know the most today but those who are prepared to keep learning tomorrow.

Equally important is strengthening the skills machines cannot replicate. AI excels at pattern recognition and prediction but it lacks empathy, cultural nuance and moral judgment. Workers who can listen, interpret and guide others through complex human situations will remain indispensable. Whether it is a teacher mentoring students, a nurse caring for patients, or a manager fostering trust within a team, the human dimensions of work will only grow more valuable as machines take over mechanical tasks.

That does not mean technical skills can be ignored. Workers need not become AI researchers but they must grow comfortable with digital tools. Understanding how AI functions, its strengths and weaknesses and how to use it responsibly will become as essential as computer literacy is today. AI literacy is likely to become a foundational requirement across industries. Even in fields such as marketing, journalism, or agriculture, workers will increasingly collaborate with AI systems to make decisions, analyze data and generate ideas.

Equally vital is cultivating a mindset of collaboration rather than rivalry. Viewing AI as a competitor risks wasted energy in resisting inevitable changes. Seeing it as a partner, however, allows workers to focus on what is most meaningful and uniquely human. The future may not belong to the fastest or strongest but to those who can orchestrate human and machine intelligence together.

There is also the question of values. Preparing for an AI-driven economy is not only about employability; it is also about ensuring that the economy itself serves human well-being. Workers who engage with ethical questions and advocate for transparency and fairness in AI deployment will shape not only their own futures but also the character of the workplace. Preparation, therefore, means acquiring skills while also influencing how technology is applied.

The greatest challenge for workers is not fear of replacement but the cultivation of adaptability, curiosity and humanity. If AI can remove drudgery, it also opens space to redefine careers around creativity, empathy and problem-solving. That future is not something to fear but something to prepare for—with open eyes and a commitment to continual growth.

WILL AI ACCELERATE THE DECLINE
OF CERTAIN PROFESSIONS, LIKE LAW,
MEDICINE, OR TEACHING?

When people wonder whether AI will accelerate the decline of professions, what is really being asked is whether machines will hollow out some of society's most respected callings. These careers have long been cornerstones of trust and expertise and the prospect of AI reshaping them stirs both excitement and unease. AI is unlikely to make these professions vanish but it could alter their scope and status in ways that feel like decline to some and transformation to others.

Consider law, where much of a lawyer's work involves research —sifting through case law, contracts and statutes to build arguments. AI excels at this kind of pattern recognition, scanning thousands of documents in seconds to uncover relevant precedents. For clients, this means faster and cheaper services. For junior lawyers and paralegals, however, it removes many of the tasks that traditionally defined the early stages of their careers. The result may be fewer entry-level opportunities and greater pressure on lawyers to distinguish themselves through strategy, persuasion and client relationships. Law will not disappear but the ladder into it may become steeper and its prestige may diminish if much of the technical expertise is outsourced to machines.

Medicine tells a similar story. AI systems can now spot tumors in scans, predict health risks from genetic data and even propose treatment plans based on vast datasets. In some cases, they surpass human doctors in accuracy; yet medicine is not only about diagnosis. It is about the conversation in the exam room, the trust between patient and provider and the navigation of values and trade-offs. AI may strip away some of the diagnostic mystique that once elevated doctors as near-oracles but it could also return medicine to its human core. Freed from paperwork and routine analysis, doctors may devote more time to listening, counseling and guiding. For those drawn to medicine for human connection, this may feel like a renaissance; for those who built their identity on specialized expertise, it may feel like diminishment.

Teaching may be the most sensitive profession of all. AI already personalizes lessons, grades assignments and provides on-demand tutoring. For parents and administrators, this suggests efficiency and equity. For teachers, it raises questions of relevance. If AI can teach algebra at each student's pace, what role does the classroom teacher serve? The likely outcome is not obsolescence but evolution. Teachers may shift toward mentoring, fostering critical thinking and cultivating social and emotional skills. These roles have always been vital but often undervalued. Ironically, AI could highlight just how irreplaceable they are. The decline, if any, may be less about teaching itself and more about the traditional lecture model, which may give way to more human-centered education.

What ties these professions together is the way AI shifts the balance between technical expertise and human qualities. When value in a profession derives primarily from knowledge recall, data analysis, or routine tasks, AI will erode it. When it derives from judgment, empathy, creativity, or trust, AI may elevate it. The professions themselves are unlikely to disappear but the mechanical aspects will fade, while the deeply human dimensions move to the forefront.

Will AI accelerate the decline of professions? In some respects, yes. Entire segments of these careers may shrink or transform beyond recognition. Yet it is equally possible to view this not as decline but as re-centering. The real challenge lies not in AI itself but in whether professions adapt quickly enough to embrace the human strengths that technology cannot replace.

HOW CAN HUMANS AND AI COLLABORATE MOST EFFECTIVELY IN THE WORKPLACE?

The conversation about AI in the workplace often swings between extremes, with some fearing machines will replace humans entirely, while others envision effortless partnership. The reality lies somewhere in between. Effective collaboration between humans and AI is less about neatly dividing tasks and more about balancing trust, oversight and complementary strengths. When that balance is struck, the workplace does not just become more efficient—it becomes more human.

The starting point is recognizing that AI is a tool, not a colleague in the human sense. It lacks intuition, values and empathy but it possesses speed and pattern recognition on a scale humans cannot match. This makes AI powerful in tasks involving data analysis, prediction, or repetitive processing. Humans, by contrast, excel at interpreting nuance, exercising judgment and navigating social and ethical contexts. Collaboration works best when AI provides the data-driven foundation and humans supply the framing, context and direction.

Consider medicine. An AI system might scan thousands of patient records and imaging results to highlight likely diagnoses but a doctor must sit with the patient, explain the findings and guide choices aligned with the patient's values. In this partnership, the AI brings breadth of data, while the human provides depth of understanding. Neither could perform as effectively alone.

The same holds true in business. AI can forecast market trends or analyze consumer behavior with remarkable accuracy but it cannot weigh the ethical implications of pricing strategies or predict how a new product will resonate culturally. That requires human imagination and judgment. The most effective collaborations do not outsource decisions to AI; they use AI to expand the range of options and insights, while relying on humans to make final choices with empathy and foresight.

Trust plays a central role. Workers must feel confident that AI systems are reliable, while also feeling empowered to question them. Blind faith in machine output risks errors or abuses but constant skepticism undermines efficiency. Building trust requires transparency: systems that explain their reasoning, managers who encourage questioning and training that equips workers to understand both the strengths and limits of AI. When people know why AI produces a recommendation, they can treat it as a partner rather than a black box.

Collaboration does not emerge automatically; workplaces must be designed to foster it. If AI is introduced solely as a cost-cutting measure, employees may view it as a rival and resist integration. If instead it is framed as a tool that removes drudgery and creates time for more meaningful tasks, collaboration becomes natural. A teacher may welcome AI systems that grade assignments if they allow more energy for mentoring and discussion. An engineer may embrace AI-driven simulations if they reduce repetitive calculations and open space for innovation.

The most effective collaborations recognize that humans and AI do not compete on the same playing field. Machines thrive on scale and precision, while humans thrive on meaning and connection. The future of work will not be about proving which is better but about orchestrating the strengths of both. When AI is treated as a partner that amplifies human abilities, the workplace becomes less about efficiency and more about creating value that neither could achieve alone.

WHAT DOES IT MEAN TO HAVE
AN AI CO-WORKER?

The phrase 'AI co-worker' may sound unusual at first. A co-worker is typically someone who chats at the coffee machine, carries quirks and moods and shares a stake in the job. AI is none of those things. It does not feel frustration or celebrate birthdays. Yet more people describe AI tools as if they were colleagues. What does that mean? It signals a rethinking of collaboration in workplaces where not all contributors are human.

Having an AI co-worker does not mean working beside a robot with a name badge. It usually means part of a workflow is handled by a system with a level of autonomy and intelligence once reserved for humans. For example, a journalist may draft an article with AI assistance for headlines, structure and fact-checking, or a project manager may rely on AI to track schedules, highlight risks and prepare reports. In such cases, AI is not just background software; it performs functions that only recently would have been assigned to human colleagues.

This shift blurs the line between tool and teammate. A spreadsheet that crunches numbers is not seen as a co-worker. But when AI suggests a marketing strategy or flags a legal risk, it feels closer to collaboration. The machine is no longer simply executing commands; it is generating ideas, anticipating needs and mimicking the give-and-take of teamwork. That can be both empowering and unsettling.

On the empowering side, an AI co-worker can handle repetitive tasks, freeing workers to focus on creativity, problem-solving and the human aspects of their roles. A teacher might welcome an AI system that grades routine assignments, allowing more time for mentoring and designing projects. In this sense, AI can feel like the most reliable colleague imaginable—always available, never tired, never distracted.

But challenges remain. Human colleagues bring context, humor and moral judgment—qualities AI lacks. Overreliance risks diminishing the richness of human collaboration. Accountability also becomes critical. If an AI system misdiagnoses a patient or suggests a flawed financial strategy, responsibility still rests with the human professional. Trusting an AI co-worker requires careful oversight, not blind delegation.

The concept of AI as a co-worker may reshape workplace relationships and hierarchies. Employees who can harness AI effectively may be seen as more valuable, while others may feel sidelined. Just as past generations learned to work with computers, today's workers must learn to team with AI—understanding its strengths, compensating for its weaknesses and integrating it into group dynamics.

Ultimately, having an AI co-worker means entering a hybrid workplace where not all contributors are human, yet the quality of human work depends on collaboration with non-human partners. It is not about replacing camaraderie with algorithms but about weaving machine intelligence into the social fabric of teams. Done well, this shift could make work more rewarding, emphasizing the parts of a job that demand human depth. Done poorly, it could leave workers feeling diminished. The outcome will depend on whether AI is treated as a silent competitor or as a partner that expands what teams can achieve together.

COULD AI IMPROVE WORKPLACE SAFETY AND REDUCE HAZARDOUS LABOR?

The connection between AI and workplace safety is one of the most promising aspects of technological change. For as long as people have worked in dangerous environments—factories, mines, oil rigs and construction sites—the question has been how to reduce risk without halting productivity. Safety regulations, protective equipment and better training have helped but accidents still occur because humans grow tired, become distracted, or cannot anticipate every hazard. AI, with its ability to monitor, predict and adapt in real time, offers a new layer of protection that could redefine what it means to feel safe at work.

One way AI contributes is through prediction. Sensors placed on heavy equipment or in high-risk environments can feed streams of data into AI systems trained to recognize danger signals. For example, an AI monitoring a factory floor might detect an unusual vibration in a machine—something a human would not notice until failure occurred. By flagging the problem early, AI can prevent accidents and avoid costly downtime. In construction, AI-powered drones can scan sites for structural weaknesses or unsafe practices, alerting supervisors before harm occurs. In this way, workplaces shift from reacting to accidents toward preventing them.

AI also reduces risk by removing humans from hazardous tasks. Mining, long one of the most dangerous industries, exposes workers to collapses, toxic substances and heavy machinery accidents. Autonomous vehicles and robotic drills, guided by AI, now perform much of this work without placing human lives in harm's way. In warehouses, AI-driven robots manage heavy lifting and repetitive motion tasks that often lead to injuries over time. The challenge, however, lies in ensuring that workers displaced by automation have opportunities to transition into safer, meaningful roles.

Workplace safety is not limited to physical hazards. AI can also address subtler risks such as fatigue and stress. Wearable devices can track workers' heart rates, posture and alertness, notifying managers if someone is at risk of exhaustion. For truck drivers and pilots, AI can detect signs of drowsiness and issue early warnings. In offices, AI tools that analyze workload patterns may identify employees at risk of burnout—a quieter but equally significant safety issue. Used responsibly, such monitoring could promote healthier environments that extend well beyond hard hats and steel-toed boots.

However, challenges remain. Safety relies on trust and workers may feel uneasy about constant monitoring. A system that tracks posture or eye movement could seem invasive without strong privacy protections. Accountability is also critical. If an AI system misses a hazard or provides faulty data, responsibility still rests with human supervisors. Employers must therefore ensure that AI complements, rather than replaces, human judgment in safety-critical decisions.

The potential benefits are profound. Construction sites could become places where scaffolds, beams and cranes are constantly cross-checked by AI against safety standards. Hospitals might prevent injuries by equipping nurses with AI-assisted lifting devices. Mines and factories could delegate their most dangerous roles to machines, allowing humans to oversee operations from safer positions.

AI has the capacity to greatly improve workplace safety and reduce hazardous labor but these outcomes will not happen automatically. They require thoughtful implementation, transparency and a commitment to protecting workers—not only from physical risks but also from over-surveillance and job displacement. If societies strike this balance, AI could not only save lives but also redefine what it means to work in a safe and dignified environment.

HOW DO WE BALANCE EFFICIENCY WITH THE NEED FOR HUMAN OVERSIGHT?

Efficiency has long been the guiding force of technological advancement: faster, cheaper, smoother—the promise every new tool appears to offer. Artificial intelligence elevates that promise to unprecedented heights. It can scan vast datasets in seconds, automate processes that once required hours and generate insights that exceed human cognitive limits. Yet alongside this surge of efficiency arises a pressing question: how can organizations ensure that, in their drive to streamline, they do not sacrifice the indispensable role of human oversight? Balancing speed with sound judgment has become one of the most delicate challenges of the AI era.

The benefits of efficiency are often self-evident. In healthcare, AI can analyze medical scans with remarkable speed, detecting signs of illness earlier than overextended radiologists might. In logistics, it can reroute shipments in real time, reducing delays and cutting costs. In finance, algorithms can identify fraudulent activity before it escalates. These gains are significant—they save time, money and even lives. However, efficiency pursued in isolation can be dangerous. Systems optimized solely for speed or profit may overlook ethical, cultural, or human dimensions. That is where oversight becomes critical.

When overregulated, AI risks becoming a bureaucratic tool, hampered by layers of approval that negate its advantages. When oversight is too weak, AI becomes a black box—making decisions that affect lives without transparency or accountability. The solution lies in striking a middle ground, where humans remain actively involved without undermining the benefits of automation. This often involves designing systems where AI manages routine tasks, while humans are empowered to make nuanced decisions—especially in gray areas where empathy, ethics and context are essential.

In aviation, for example, autopilot systems outperform human pilots at maintaining altitude and speed. Yet few would argue that pilots are obsolete. Their presence becomes vital during emergencies, when intuition and adaptability outweigh mechanical precision. A similar model may be needed in other domains: delegate the predictable to machines and preserve the human role for the complex and consequential.

Transparency is essential to this balance. Oversight can only function when human agents understand how and why AI systems make decisions. If algorithms are too opaque, oversight devolves into a meaningless formality. Embedding explainability into AI design—tools that allow humans to trace the logic behind each recommendation—is not a luxury but a necessity. Effective oversight is not about mistrusting machines; it is about ensuring that machine logic remains aligned with human values.

A cultural shift is also necessary. Organizations must resist the impulse to idolize efficiency above all else. Human oversight requires time and resources and in environments driven by profit, it may seem like an impediment. Yet the long-term consequences of neglecting oversight—loss of trust, ethical violations and systemic failures—are far more costly. A sustainable culture of innovation must celebrate efficiency without allowing it to eclipse accountability.

Ultimately, efficiency and oversight are not opposing forces. When properly integrated, they reinforce one another. Oversight ensures that efficiency is pursued responsibly; efficiency ensures that oversight remains manageable and scalable. AI offers powerful tools that can make the world faster and smarter—but only if society remembers that speed without judgment is not progress. It is risk. In the age of AI, success will not be measured by how rapidly decisions are made but by how wisely.

WILL AI WIDEN THE GAP BETWEEN HIGH-SKILLED AND LOW-SKILLED WORKERS?

The question of whether AI will widen the gap between high-skilled and low-skilled workers is one of the most pressing concerns for the future of work. Technology has always redistributed opportunity—sometimes lifting people into new roles and sometimes leaving others behind. With AI, the pace of redistribution is much faster, raising the stakes. The concern is that those with education, technical expertise and access to resources will thrive, while those in routine roles may be pushed further to the margins.

AI tends to reward workers who can use it effectively. Someone who knows how to prompt an AI system, interpret its outputs and apply them strategically becomes far more productive. A lawyer using AI to analyze case law can build arguments faster than one who does not. A marketer who leverages AI tools to refine campaigns can reach audiences more effectively. These workers not only keep their jobs; they increase their value. By contrast, the warehouse worker whose tasks are automated or the customer service representative replaced by a chatbot may find fewer opportunities unless retraining is available. This contrast alone suggests a widening gap.

This dynamic is not new. When computers entered offices in the 1980s and 1990s, workers who adapted prospered while others struggled. But AI raises the intensity by encroaching on both manual and cognitive work. Jobs once thought insulated—clerical work, basic analysis, or simple reporting—are now within reach of AI systems. This puts pressure on the middle of the labor market, where many stable jobs once resided. Without intervention, economies could polarize, with high-skilled workers commanding greater rewards and low-skilled workers pushed toward unstable or lower-paying roles.

Still, the gap is not inevitable. Much depends on how accessible AI tools become and how societies support reskilling. If AI remains expensive or concentrated in the hands of a few, inequality will grow. But if the tools are democratized—easy to use, affordable and integrated into education—they could help lower-skilled workers advance. A small business owner without formal marketing training can now design ads and analyze customer behavior with AI. A nurse's aide might use AI to track patient vitals more effectively. In such cases, AI acts as an equalizer, giving people without advanced degrees access to capabilities once requiring years of training.

The role of business is crucial. If AI is treated primarily as a cost-cutting measure to replace low-skilled labor, the gap will grow. If instead it is used to augment workers—helping them take on new responsibilities and develop new skills—the outcome could look very different. Governments also play a role, creating policies that encourage training programs, apprenticeships and safety nets to ease the transition.

At its core, the question is not only whether AI widens the gap but whether society allows it to. Left to market forces alone, it likely will, since the technology favors those already positioned to use it well. But with deliberate choices—making AI literacy universal, creating pathways for workers to move into new roles and designing systems that augment rather than replace—inequality can be reduced rather than deepened.

So, will AI widen the gap? If history is a guide, it likely will at first. But the final outcome depends on how intentionally societies prepare for the shift. The divide is not destiny; it is a challenge that collective imagination and policy can help close.

COULD AI REDUCE GLOBAL INEQUALITY BY PROVIDING ACCESS TO TOOLS AND KNOWLEDGE

It is an intriguing question: instead of deepening divides, could AI actually reduce global inequality by giving more people access to tools and knowledge once locked behind borders, wealth, or privilege? The possibility is real but as with most technologies, the outcome depends on how it is developed and distributed. AI has the potential to be a great equalizer, yet it could just as easily reinforce old hierarchies if left unchecked.

At its best, AI can make expertise widely available. A farmer in rural Kenya might use an AI-powered app to diagnose crop diseases that previously required expensive agronomists. A student in a small town in India could access AI tutoring systems that adjust to their learning pace, even if the local school is underfunded. A small business owner in Latin America may design marketing campaigns or financial models with AI tools that rival what large corporations once paid consultants to create. In such cases, AI is not replacing local effort; it is amplifying it and lowering barriers that separate people from opportunity.

Knowledge has always been one of the most powerful levers for equality. Historically, access to advanced training, specialized advice, or cutting-edge research was limited to wealthy regions and elite institutions. AI changes this. Large language models can summarize complex information, explain scientific concepts and translate across dozens of languages instantly. For communities long excluded from the global knowledge economy, such access can be transformative. A young entrepreneur with an internet connection can now receive guidance once dependent on mentorship from well-connected insiders.

Yet caveats remain. Access to AI still depends on infrastructure —electricity, reliable internet and digital devices. Many regions lack these basics, meaning AI could deepen rather than close the divide between connected and disconnected communities. Cost is another factor. If the most powerful AI systems remain expensive and controlled by a handful of companies, they will primarily serve the wealthy, leaving low-income groups with weaker versions. True democratization requires intentional policies, open-source development and affordable access to ensure benefits spread broadly.

Cultural relevance also matters. An AI trained mainly on Western data may not fully reflect or serve the needs of users in other contexts. Genuine democratization involves building systems that capture diverse perspectives and languages, empowering communities to preserve and share their own traditions rather than only consuming imported knowledge.

Perhaps most importantly, AI must be delivered in ways that grant agency. When communities can adapt the technology to local needs, it can spark bottom-up innovation—solving problems outsiders might never consider, from climate challenges to indigenous language preservation. If, instead, AI arrives as a one-size-fits-all product designed elsewhere, it risks reinforcing dependency rather than empowerment.

So, could AI reduce global inequality? Yes but only if it is paired with commitments to access, affordability, diversity and local agency. Technology alone does not rewrite power structures; it magnifies human choices about who uses it, who controls it and whose voices shape it. AI could be remembered as the tool that opened doors for billions—or as another innovation that mostly benefited those already ahead. The outcome will depend less on algorithms themselves and more on the collective will to share their benefits broadly.

WHAT ROLE MIGHT UNIVERSAL BASIC INCOME PLAY IN AN AI-TRANSFORMED ECONOMY?

The idea of universal basic income (UBI) has been discussed for decades but it feels more urgent in conversations about an AI-transformed economy. The concept is simple: every citizen receives a regular payment from the government, no strings attached, to cover basic needs. For much of modern history, it seemed like a thought experiment rather than a serious policy. But as AI threatens to automate increasing varieties of work, UBI has moved from the fringes of debate to the center. The question is no longer whether it is radical but whether it might become necessary.

The appeal of UBI in an AI-driven world lies in the disruption AI is likely to cause in labor markets. If machines can manage routine office work, much of manufacturing and even parts of professions such as law and medicine, then millions of jobs could shift or vanish. For displaced workers, retraining is one option but not everyone can transition easily. UBI steps in as a safety net, ensuring that people can still meet basic needs while economies adjust. In that sense, it is not only an economic tool but also a way of preserving social stability in times of upheaval.

Yet UBI is about more than cushioning the blow. Advocates see it as a chance to redefine the relationship between work and dignity. In a world where machines generate abundance, tying survival to employment may begin to feel outdated. With a guaranteed income floor, people could pursue work for meaning rather than necessity. An artist could create without fear of poverty. A caregiver could devote time to family without financial penalty. An entrepreneur could take risks without the threat of collapse. AI may free society from drudgery and UBI could make that freedom sustainable.

Critics, however, point to challenges. Funding UBI at scale is expensive and governments would need to rethink taxation, possibly targeting wealth generated by AI-driven corporations. Others worry about incentives: would people still work if income were guaranteed? Evidence from trials in Finland and Canada suggests most people continue working but with less stress and improved well-being. Rather than reducing motivation, UBI may cultivate a healthier, more innovative workforce. Still, cultural resistance to 'something for nothing' remains strong in many societies and could be as formidable a barrier as the economics.

It is also worth considering that UBI may not be the only solution. Some argue that targeted measures—such as wage subsidies, job guarantees, or sector-specific retraining—could be more efficient. Others see UBI as one element of a broader policy toolkit, not a silver bullet but one instrument among many to manage the transition to an AI economy.

The larger issue is that UBI compels societies to confront a fundamental question: what is the purpose of work in a world where survival no longer depends on it? If AI enables sufficient production with less human labor, then the economy will not collapse; it will evolve. UBI could serve as a bridge to that evolution, ensuring people are not left behind as societies rethink how contribution and success are defined.

Ultimately, universal basic income in an AI-driven economy is less about distributing money than about reimagining the social contract. It represents a shift from tying dignity to employment toward tying dignity to citizenship itself. Whether societies adopt it will depend not only on economics but also on values. If the belief takes hold that, in an age of machine abundance, every human deserves a baseline of security, then UBI could become one of the defining institutions of the AI era.

HOW DO WE PREVENT CONCENTRATION
OF AI POWER IN THE HANDS OF
A FEW CORPORATIONS?

One of the biggest questions about the future of AI has less to do with the technology itself and more to do with who controls it. At present, the most advanced systems are being developed by a small number of corporations with deep pockets and vast computing resources. On one level, this makes sense: such projects require massive investments in hardware, data and expertise. But it also raises concerns. If only a handful of companies control the most powerful AI tools, the benefits may be unevenly distributed and the risks magnified. Preventing this concentration of power is as much a political and social challenge as it is a technical one.

The danger of concentration is straightforward. If a few corporations dominate AI, they gain the power to determine who has access, which applications are developed, how data is used and whose values are embedded in the systems. This could stifle innovation, as smaller players would struggle to compete. It could also deepen inequality, with wealth and influence flowing to corporations while ordinary people have little say in how the technology shapes their lives. History shows how quickly monopolies distort markets. With AI, the stakes are even higher, because we are not just talking about markets but also about the structures of work, governance and knowledge.

One path forward is regulation. Governments can ensure that no single company enjoys unchecked control over AI. Options include antitrust actions to limit monopolistic power, transparency requirements compelling disclosure of how models function and data-sharing mandates that give smaller organizations a chance to compete. The challenge lies in balance:

regulate too little and corporate dominance may prevail; regulate too much and innovation could be stifled or driven underground. The balance point will vary across countries but the principle is constant—AI is too important to be left entirely in private hands.

Another approach is open access. A growing movement supports open-source AI models that anyone can study, adapt and deploy. While often less powerful than proprietary systems, these models are improving rapidly. Open access democratizes innovation, enabling startups, researchers and even individuals to participate without billions in capital. Of course, openness carries risks, since bad actors can use these systems as easily as good ones. Yet if the alternative is a world in which only a few corporations decide what is possible, the risks of openness may be worth bearing.

Public investment is also essential. Universities, non-profits and international coalitions can pool resources to create AI that serves the public good. Imagine treating AI as societies treat public health or basic science: too important to be left solely to private interests. Publicly funded projects could prioritize applications that corporations might overlook as unprofitable, such as tools for underserved communities or support for less widely spoken languages.

Preventing the concentration of power is not only about laws or code; it is also about expectations. If citizens demand transparency, accountability and fair access, companies and governments will feel pressure to respond. If the public remains passive, power will naturally flow to those already best positioned to seize it.

So, how can the concentration of AI power be prevented? By treating AI not just as a technological breakthrough but as a societal resource. That requires a combination of effective regulation, support for open alternatives, public investment and civic engagement. The stakes could not be higher. AI will influence how economies function, how knowledge spreads and how decisions are made. If it remains concentrated in the hands of a few, the future may be narrowed to their vision alone. If it is shared more widely, it could reflect the values, needs and creativity of humanity as a whole.

HOW WILL AI AFFECT THE SENSE OF IDENTITY PEOPLE DERIVE FROM THEIR WORK?

For a long time, work has been one of the strongest anchors of identity. People introduce themselves with job titles, children are asked what they want to be when they grow up and careers often shape not only how others see them but also how they see themselves. In an AI-driven world, that anchor is beginning to shift. If AI takes on tasks that once defined entire professions, people may question not only their roles but also the deeper sense of who they are.

Part of this comes from the changing nature of expertise. A doctor, for example, has long been viewed as someone who can diagnose illness through years of study and intuition. If an AI can scan thousands of medical records and identify conditions more accurately than a human, then the meaning of being a doctor changes. The role may become less about ultimate expertise and more about guiding, communicating and partnering in decision-making. This is not necessarily a loss but it does alter how individuals identify with their professions. What once felt like mastery may now resemble stewardship.

For others, identity may erode more painfully. Workers in roles that AI automates away—such as clerical staff, drivers, or call center employees—often draw pride from being reliable and efficient. If those roles vanish or diminish, individuals may feel discarded, not just economically but also personally. Losing a job can mean losing a piece of self. In this way, AI's disruption is not only about employment numbers but also about dignity, belonging and self-worth.

On the other hand, AI opens opportunities to reimagine identity in positive ways. Freed from routine tasks, workers may rediscover aspects of their roles that align more closely with their values. A teacher no longer burdened by grading might see their identity shift toward that of a mentor and role model. An architect who uses AI to generate endless design options may focus more on vision, storytelling and human impact. In such cases, AI does not erase identity; it sharpens it, emphasizing the parts of work that feel most human.

There is also the possibility of entirely new identities emerging. As AI creates new categories of work, people may define themselves by roles that do not yet exist. Just as nobody a century ago could claim to be a software engineer or data scientist, future generations may take pride in jobs such as AI ethicist, human-AI interaction designer, or experience curator. Identity adapts as work evolves, though it often takes time for culture to recognize and respect new fields.

The deeper question is whether societies can help people detach identity from employment altogether. If AI enables a world where fewer people need traditional jobs, identity may come more from creativity, relationships, or community roles rather than careers. This would mark a profound cultural shift, moving away from the idea that identity is tied to what people do toward the idea that it is tied to who they are. That vision excites some and unsettles others, especially in cultures where work has long been tied to morality and worth.

So, how will AI affect the sense of identity derived from work? It will unsettle it, reshape it and in some cases, liberate it. For some, the loss of familiar roles will feel like diminishment. For others, the re-centering of work around human qualities will feel like enrichment. The challenge ahead lies not only in creating new kinds of jobs but also in nurturing new ways for people to find meaning—in what they do and perhaps even more importantly, in who they are beyond what they do.

COULD WIDESPREAD AUTOMATION LEAD TO A CRISIS OF PURPOSE FOR MANY INDIVIDUALS?

It is not difficult to envision a future in which widespread automation leads many individuals to ask, 'What am I for?' For generations, work has been a central structure through which people organize their lives and derive a sense of purpose. It provides income, certainly but it also offers rhythm, community and the affirmation of being needed. If machines assume control of tasks once considered essential, there is a genuine risk that individuals will face a crisis of purpose—even when their material needs are met.

This concern is not new. When industrial machinery replaced artisanal craftsmanship, many skilled workers felt their identities eroded. When office automation reduced clerical roles, some experienced a sense of devaluation. What sets artificial intelligence apart is the breadth and depth of its disruption—it affects not only physical labor but also intellectual and creative domains. If an AI system can compose music, draft legal briefs, or manage financial portfolios, the activities once regarded as markers of human excellence may seem diminished. For those whose identities are deeply tied to such expertise, the threat is not merely economic but existential.

A crisis of purpose often emerges when individuals equate their worth solely with their labor. If societal values continue to conflate productivity with personal value, automation will be especially devastating. Those whose jobs disappear may feel not only unemployed but unnecessary. This sense of displacement can foster isolation, depression and resentment—particularly in communities where work is central to cultural identity. The resulting danger is not only personal despair but also broader social unrest, as entire groups feel stripped of meaning and place.

Yet automation also presents an opportunity. By removing repetitive and menial labor, it creates the potential for individuals to pursue alternative sources of purpose—such as creativity, lifelong learning, caregiving, or civic engagement. Purpose may begin to shift from economic productivity toward personal and communal fulfillment. However, this transformation requires a profound cultural shift and such shifts are rarely smooth. Redefining identity outside traditional employment may prove especially difficult in societies where career is tightly linked to self-worth.

Institutional response will be critical. Education systems can promote curiosity, adaptability and lifelong learning, preparing individuals for evolving definitions of purpose. Governments might explore safety nets such as universal basic income to decouple survival from employment, enabling people to seek meaning beyond the workplace. Employers can also reframe roles to emphasize distinct human capacities—creativity, empathy and moral judgment—ensuring that workers continue to feel valued, even in AI-augmented environments. Without these strategic shifts, automation may erode the very foundation of meaning for millions.

Generational differences will also influence the transition. Younger individuals, raised amid rapid technological change, may more readily detach identity from stable, long-term careers. They may find purpose in flexible roles, side projects, or virtual communities. Older generations, having built their lives on stable employment models, may face a more disorienting adjustment. Bridging this generational divide will be vital to maintaining social cohesion in an era of profound change.

Automation does carry the potential to trigger a crisis of purpose. The risk is real and must not be underestimated. Yet the outcome will depend less on technological capability and more on human choices. If societies cling to outdated narratives that equate labor with value, the crisis will arrive. But if this moment is seized as an opportunity to redefine purpose—expanding it to include creativity, connection, growth and service—then what now appears to be a threat may, in hindsight, be seen as a turning point toward a deeper, more inclusive understanding of what it means to lead a meaningful life.

MIGHT AI ALLOW PEOPLE TO PURSUE PROJECTS OF PASSION INSTEAD OF TRADITIONAL JOBS?

For many people, passion projects exist on the sidelines of life. Someone might write poetry at night after a long day of office work or volunteer in their community on weekends. These pursuits often do not pay the bills, which is why they remain hobbies.

If AI reshapes the economy in ways that weaken the link between survival and employment—whether through higher productivity, universal basic income, or new forms of wealth distribution—people may find themselves free to elevate these side pursuits into central parts of their lives. The novelist who never had time to finish a manuscript, the tinkerer who dreamed of inventing a new device, or the caregiver who longed to focus on family could all see their lives transformed.

This shift could be especially powerful in creative fields. AI can already draft stories, compose music and generate visual art. Some fear this will replace human artists but another way to view it is as collaboration. A songwriter could use AI to experiment with chord progressions never before imagined. A filmmaker might generate endless concept art in minutes, freeing more time for storytelling. In this sense, AI may not erase passion projects but accelerate them, turning dreams into reality at a pace once impossible.

Still, pursuing passion projects is not as simple as handing off drudgery to machines. Purpose often requires discipline, effort and even struggle. If people suddenly have endless free time, not everyone will know how to fill it. Some may drift, uncertain of what matters without the structure of a traditional job. That is where culture and education play a role. Societies must cultivate not just technical skills but also the capacity to explore, reflect and create. Passion often emerges through trial and error, through small experiments that gradually grow into something larger.

Equity is another concern. If only a privileged few gain the security to pursue passion projects while others struggle to survive, the promise of AI will ring hollow. For AI to unlock human potential, access to its benefits must be broad. That requires affordable tools, fair distribution of wealth and support systems that encourage exploration. Otherwise, passion projects risk becoming luxuries rather than lifelines.

The potential, however, is enormous. Imagine a society where millions of people channel their energy into writing, science, caregiving, or community building—not because they have to but because they want to. Some projects may remain small and personal, while others ripple outward to transform communities. In all of this, AI could act as the quiet collaborator, handling background work so humans can fully embrace curiosity and creativity.

Ultimately, AI may allow passion projects to move from the margins to the center of human life. But the transformation will not come from machines alone. It will depend on whether societies use this freedom wisely—whether they drift aimlessly or embrace it to enrich individuals and communities. The answer to that question may determine whether the AI era is remembered as one of emptiness or one of flourishing.

HOW DO WE REDEFINE SUCCESS IN A WORLD WHERE AI HANDLES MUCH OF THE LABOR?

For much of modern history, success has been tightly tied to work. Individuals are often judged by their careers, income, titles and productivity. The cultural shorthand for success has frequently been the size of a paycheck or the prestige of a position. But what happens when artificial intelligence takes over much of the labor that once defined these metrics? As machines become faster and often more capable, traditional measures of success begin to lose their relevance. In this new context, redefining success becomes less about competing with machines and more about asking what it truly means to live a good life.

One emerging possibility is a shift from measuring output to valuing impact. Rather than counting hours worked or products created, success might be assessed by the difference an individual makes in the lives of others. A teacher could be valued not for the number of lessons delivered but for the curiosity sparked in students. A community leader may be recognized not for administrative output but for the strength of the networks they foster. In this way, success moves away from efficiency and toward influence.

Creativity may also become a central benchmark. As AI takes on repetitive and rules-based tasks, the human contribution may lie in originality and vision. Success could be linked to the ability to imagine, to connect ideas in novel ways, or to tell stories that resonate across cultures and generations.

This does not suggest that everyone will become an artist but it does imply that creative expression—whether in writing, design, or civic innovation—may carry greater cultural weight. In such a world, success could be defined by the authenticity and uniqueness of human insight and contribution.

Another potential transformation lies in the revaluation of balance over sacrifice. For decades, working long hours has been treated as a badge of honor. But if AI assumes more of the heavy lifting, societies may begin to appreciate the ability to balance work with relationships, health and personal growth. A culture could emerge in which success is reflected in the capacity to care for family, engage with community and pursue learning or leisure, rather than climb a relentless career ladder. This would represent a profound cultural realignment—one made possible by the freedoms AI unlocks.

Redefining success will not come easily. Cultural habits are deeply embedded and societies are often slow to relinquish measures such as wealth or social status. It is also possible that AI may widen inequality, with some continuing to chase material definitions of success while others explore more holistic alternatives. This divergence could create cultural rifts, dividing those who remain anchored to traditional metrics from those pioneering broader understandings of fulfillment. The outcome may rest on how intentionally institutions, education systems and communities guide the public conversation.

At its core, success in an AI-driven world may come to focus less on what individuals produce and more on who they become. Are they kind? Are they curious? Do they strengthen families, nurture healthier communities and contribute to a more livable planet? These metrics may seem softer than profit margins or productivity statistics but they may ultimately prove more enduring. As AI handles increasing amounts of labor, humanity may reclaim success as a reflection of meaning, connection and contribution.

Ultimately, in a world where machines take on much of the work, success may no longer be defined by being busier, richer, or faster. It may be measured instead by how deeply individuals engage with their humanity. If societies embrace that redefinition, the age of AI might be remembered not as the end of work but as the beginning of a richer, more meaningful understanding of what it truly means to succeed.

COULD AI MAKE THE 4-DAY WORKWEEK OR EVEN THE END OF THE WORKWEEK POSSIBLE?

The dream of a shorter workweek is not new. For decades, people have speculated that as technology increased productivity, fewer hours would be needed to achieve the same results. In the early 20th century, the five-day, 40-hour workweek became standard in many countries—a major improvement over the grueling six-day weeks of the industrial age. The assumption was that rising productivity would lead to shorter workweeks, yet many societies instead reinforced longer working hours.

Now, with AI accelerating productivity in ways that dwarf earlier technologies, the idea of a four-day workweek—or even the dissolution of the workweek as we know it—feels more plausible than ever.

AI could make the four-day workweek viable by stripping away inefficiencies. Much of modern work is tied to routine tasks such as data entry, report writing, scheduling and compliance paperwork—precisely the areas where AI excels. If those tasks are automated or streamlined, the total hours required to achieve the same business outcomes could drop significantly. An accountant might complete in three days what once required five, or a marketing team might produce campaigns in half the time using AI-driven tools. The productivity gain is real but whether it translates into shorter hours depends on cultural and managerial choices.

History suggests that productivity gains do not automatically lead to reduced hours. More often, they translate into greater output, higher profits and in some cases, added pressure on workers to deliver faster. For AI to enable a four-day workweek, employers would need to choose to pass efficiency gains back to employees as time, rather than capturing them solely as revenue. Experiments with shorter workweeks have already shown promising results, often yielding not only happier employees but also equal or greater productivity. AI could strengthen that case, making old schedules difficult to justify when the work itself requires less time.

The more radical idea is the dissolution of the workweek altogether—the possibility that AI could automate so extensively that humans no longer need to work in traditional ways. This scenario may be distant but not impossible. If machines can meet the bulk of societies' material needs, the structure of Monday-to-Friday employment could become obsolete. Work might shift toward intermittent projects, creative pursuits, or fields where human judgment and empathy remain essential. The very concept of a weekend could blur, with time divided more fluidly among creation, leisure and community.

Significant hurdles remain. Economies are built not only on productivity but also on cultural norms. Many people still equate long hours with dedication and some industries continue to prize face time over efficiency. Governments and corporations would need to rethink policies, incentives and taxation to make shorter workweeks sustainable. Equity is another concern: will shorter schedules extend to all workers, or only to knowledge professionals with access to AI? If the benefits of automation are unevenly distributed, society could split between those enjoying expanded leisure and those trapped in traditional routines.

So, could AI make the four-day workweek—or even the end of the workweek—possible? Yes but it will not happen by default. Achieving that future requires intentional choices by businesses, policymakers and workers to ensure that productivity gains translate into time, not merely profits. The potential rewards are vast: more time for families, creativity, rest and community. Whether that vision is realized depends less on AI's capabilities and more on the choices societies make with the freedom it provides.

HOW WILL AI INFLUENCE THE FUTURE
OF UNIONS AND WORKER RIGHTS?

Unions have always risen in response to shifts in how people work. In the industrial era, they fought for safer factories, shorter hours and fair pay. In the information age, they adapted to protect service and knowledge workers. Now, as AI reshapes the workplace, unions once again face the challenge of redefining their purpose. The influence of AI on unions and worker rights is likely to be profound—not because unions will disappear but because the nature of what they fight for will evolve.

One of the most immediate pressures AI introduces is job security. As routine and even some skilled tasks are automated, workers may feel vulnerable to displacement. In earlier eras, unions rallied to protect jobs from outsourcing or mechanization. With AI, the threat is not another workforce abroad but machines performing tasks faster and more cheaply. This creates a new kind of tension: unions are no longer negotiating against rival workers but against algorithms. This shift may push unions to advocate more strongly for retraining programs, job transition support and guarantees that the productivity gains from AI are shared with workers rather than captured entirely by corporations.

AI also raises new issues of surveillance and fairness. Many companies are already experimenting with systems that track worker performance, monitor keystrokes, or evaluate efficiency in real-time. While employers may argue that such monitoring improves productivity, workers may view it as intrusive or dehumanizing. In this space, unions could play a critical role in setting boundaries, negotiating for transparency in how AI systems are used and ensuring that workers are not reduced to data points in machine-driven evaluations. Protecting dignity and privacy may become as central to union advocacy as protecting wages once was.

Bargaining power is another concern. If AI enables companies to operate with fewer employees, unions could see their leverage weakened as memberships decline. Yet there is also a counter-possibility: if unions adapt quickly, they could become influential voices in shaping how AI is deployed. Unions could negotiate not just for higher pay but for co-ownership of AI-driven productivity gains, or demand that workers have representation in decisions about automation. In this sense, AI could spur unions to become more innovative, redefining collective bargaining for a digital age.

On a global level, AI may encourage new forms of worker solidarity. Because AI systems can be deployed across borders, the challenges workers face may become increasingly universal. A driver in one country and a driver in another could both be threatened by self-driving vehicles. A call center worker in Asia and one in North America might both be displaced by the same chatbot. This shared vulnerability could encourage unions to think less locally and more globally, pushing for labor standards that transcend national boundaries.

Ultimately, AI will not eliminate the need for unions; it may make them more essential. Worker rights in an AI-driven economy will extend beyond wages and hours to encompass questions of dignity, oversight, privacy and the fair distribution of automation's gains. The challenge for unions will be to modernize their strategies and language so they remain relevant to workers whose struggles differ greatly from those of the factory floor. If they succeed, they may not only survive but play a crucial role in shaping a fairer and more human-centered future of work.

WHAT ROLE WILL AI PLAY IN GLOBAL SUPPLY CHAINS AND THE CONCEPT OF 'ESSENTIAL'

AI is already reshaping the invisible backbone of modern life: global supply chains. These complex networks move raw materials, food, medicine and manufactured goods across the planet. They are systems most people rarely notice until they falter, as seen during the pandemic when shortages of masks, microchips and basic groceries revealed their fragility. The question of how AI will influence supply chains—and how societies define what is essential—goes to the heart of economic security and resilience in the years ahead.

One of AI's most immediate contributions is prediction. Supply chains rely on anticipating demand and balancing it with production and transportation. Historically, forecasts were based on past patterns and human judgment. AI can process far more data in real-time, drawing from weather reports, shipping logs, consumer behavior and geopolitical trends. This makes it possible to forecast not only what people will need but also where bottlenecks are likely to occur. A system might even warn weeks in advance of a looming shortage of a critical material, giving companies and governments time to adapt before shelves go empty.

AI also enhances resilience by rerouting goods when disruptions strike. If a port closes due to a strike or a storm, AI can instantly model alternative routes and weigh trade-offs in cost, time and risk. This is particularly important for essential goods such as food, energy and medicine. In the past, disruptions often cascaded because human planners could not react quickly enough. With AI, supply chains can become more adaptive, less fragile and better prepared for shocks.

Yet AI does more than optimize logistics—it reshapes the very idea of what counts as essential. During the pandemic, governments scrambled to decide which jobs, products and services were vital to keep society functioning. AI could make that process more precise. By mapping dependencies across industries, it could reveal how something seemingly minor—like a rare chemical used in semiconductor production—turns out to be indispensable for countless other goods. This may push societies to rethink resilience, stockpiling and the balance between local and global production. Essential may come to mean not just what is visible to the consumer but also the hidden links that sustain entire systems.

Of course, risks remain. AI-driven efficiency could tempt companies to push supply chains closer to the edge, reducing costs but leaving less margin for error. A system optimized to perfection may prove highly vulnerable if conditions shift unexpectedly. There is also the danger of concentration. If only a few corporations control the AI systems that manage global supply chains, commerce becomes dependent on their decisions, transparency and security. A cyberattack or system failure in such a scenario could ripple worldwide.

On the other hand, AI could democratize resilience. Smaller nations or companies that once lacked the capacity to model complex logistics may gain access to AI tools that level the playing field. This could reduce regional inequality, promote a more balanced global economy and enable governments and consumers alike to make more informed choices about sourcing, sustainability and risk.

In the end, AI will not only streamline supply chains but also redefine what societies consider essential. It may encourage a shift from just-in-time efficiency to just-in-case preparedness, blending speed with resilience. Perhaps the most profound change will be cultural: supply chains may no longer be seen as invisible background systems but as vital lifelines shaped by choices about technology, fairness and security. In this sense, AI will not simply manage supply chains—it will help redefine what societies cannot afford to live without.

COULD AI MANAGE ENTIRE ORGANIZATIONS OR GOVERNMENTS WITHOUT HUMAN OVERSIGHT?

The idea of AI managing entire organizations—or even governments—without human oversight sounds like the plot of a science fiction novel. Yet as AI grows more capable, it is worth asking seriously whether such a scenario could unfold. After all, AI can already coordinate complex logistics, analyze enormous datasets and make recommendations that sometimes surpass human judgment. Couldn't those same abilities be scaled up to run a company, a city, or even a nation?

Technically, the answer is yes, to some extent. AI is excellent at optimization. It could balance supply and demand within an organization, manage resources more efficiently than human bureaucracies and even simulate the outcomes of different policies before they're enacted. In theory, an AI system could monitor economic indicators, healthcare data, environmental conditions and infrastructure needs, then allocate budgets and make decisions with fewer errors or delays than human politicians or executives. For those frustrated by inefficiency or corruption, the appeal of a machine-led government can seem obvious.

But the deeper truth is that organizations and governments are not only about efficiency; they are about values, priorities and human trade-offs. An AI might determine the most cost-effective way to run a hospital system but who decides whether to prioritize cost over patient comfort? An AI could design tax policies that maximize revenue but should it also consider fairness, cultural values, or historical context? These are not technical questions; they are human ones. Without oversight, AI might follow logic that is internally consistent yet socially disastrous.

Accountability is another critical issue. In a democracy, citizens can vote leaders out of office if they disapprove of their choices.

In companies, boards can replace CEOs. But if an AI system makes a harmful decision, who bears responsibility—the engineers who built it, the leaders who implemented it, or the machine itself? Without human oversight, accountability evaporates and with it the trust that organizations and governments depend upon.

Adaptability presents a further challenge. Human beings may be messy, emotional and sometimes irrational but they also bring intuition and creativity to governance. They can sense when a population is growing restless, when a decision will spark outrage, or when compromise is more important than efficiency. AI, for all its power, struggles with the unpredictability of human culture and behavior. A government or company run entirely by algorithms might miss the subtle cues that signal discontent or the need for a softer touch.

This does not mean AI has no role. On the contrary, AI will likely become an indispensable partner in governance and management. It can highlight inefficiencies, model outcomes and surface insights that humans might miss; in disaster response, for instance, AI could coordinate relief efforts with extraordinary speed. In city planning, it could simulate traffic, housing and energy needs decades into the future. But in every case, the final decisions must remain in human hands, because governance is not only about what works but also about what matters.

So, could AI manage entire organizations or governments without human oversight? Technically, pieces of it, yes. But should it? Almost certainly not. The role of AI in leadership is best understood as augmentation, not replacement. It can help societies see farther, decide faster and act more efficiently—but the compass that tells us where to go must remain human. Otherwise, there is the risk of building perfectly optimized systems that forget the messy, contradictory and deeply human heart of governance and leadership.

ULTIMATELY, WILL AI LIBERATE HUMANITY FROM WORK OR TETHER US MORE TIGHTLY TO NEW FORMS OF LABOR?

The ultimate question about AI and work is whether it will set humanity free or bind it even more tightly. On one side of the argument, AI appears to be a liberator. If machines perform the bulk of routine, dangerous, or monotonous tasks, humans could spend more time on creativity, leisure, relationships and personal growth. On the other side, history offers a cautionary tale. Every major technological leap has promised to reduce toil, yet often it has merely reshaped it. Productivity rises but so do expectations. Instead of fewer hours, workers sometimes find themselves tethered to new systems, new responsibilities and greater pressure. AI may prove no different.

There is a compelling case for liberation. One vision of the future depicts AI handling the dull mechanics of life: processing taxes, scheduling appointments, monitoring health and managing supply chains. In such a society, survival would no longer depend on grinding through repetitive labor. People could focus on passion projects, community, or exploration. This would echo the vision of philosophers who dreamed of a society where technology provided abundance and humans devoted themselves to higher pursuits. Some even argue that universal basic income or other redistributive policies could allow AI-driven productivity to fund this shift, creating a world where employment becomes a choice rather than a necessity.

But there is also a persuasive case for tethering. Technology rarely arrives in a vacuum; it enters systems already shaped by power and profit. Employers might use AI not to shorten workweeks but to extract more productivity from each worker. Already, AI tools are being used for surveillance—tracking keystrokes, monitoring attention and evaluating performance in real-time. In this version of the future, AI does not free people from labor; it intensifies it, making workers feel constantly measured against machine efficiency. Far from liberation, it could resemble a new form of digital constraint.

The reality may lie somewhere in between. Some people, particularly those in creative or highly skilled roles, may find AI liberating. It could act as a partner that expands their capabilities, allowing them to accomplish in hours what once took days. For others, especially those in vulnerable or routine jobs, AI could mean displacement or stricter oversight. Whether AI leads to freedom or constraint may depend less on the technology itself and more on the social choices surrounding its use. Will productivity gains be broadly shared or hoarded by the few? Will workers have a voice in how AI is integrated, or will it be imposed from the top down?

There is also a psychological dimension. Even if AI reduces the necessity of traditional jobs, not everyone will feel liberated. For many, work provides structure and identity. Stripping that away without offering alternative sources of meaning could leave some adrift. Others, however, may seize the opportunity to redefine their lives around curiosity, creativity, relationships, or service. Liberation is not only about hours worked but about how individuals reimagine purpose once the old rhythms of labor shift.

So, will AI liberate humanity from work or tether it to new forms of labor? Likely both. For some, it will feel like emancipation from drudgery; for others, it may resemble confinement within ever-evolving systems of control. The decisive factor will not be the machines themselves but the values and policies guiding their use. If societies treat AI as a tool to expand human freedom, it may deliver on the promise of liberation. If not, it could deepen the very pressures it was meant to relieve. The future, as always, will not be written by the technology alone; it will be written by the choices societies make about how to live with it.

CONCLUSION

Artificial Intelligence is not coming for your job—it's changing what your job can be.

As we've seen throughout this guide, AI is a tool: powerful, yes but not a replacement for human creativity, judgment and adaptability. Those who thrive in the AI-integrated workplace won't be the ones with the most technical skills but the ones most willing to learn, evolve and collaborate with technology rather than fear it.

Whether you're in marketing, finance, education, logistics or any other field, the principles remain the same: stay curious, stay adaptable and don't stop investing in your own development. Learn how to leverage AI tools, not just to save time but to create new value. Focus on the human strength's machines can't replicate—empathy, critical thinking, ethical judgment and emotional intelligence.

The future of work belongs to those who can work *with* machines, not against them.

If there's one message to take away from this book, it's this: job security in the AI era isn't about clinging to the past—it's about preparing for what's next. That preparation doesn't require you to become a programmer. It requires you to become a learner. A strategist. A human who knows their worth and learns how to multiply it through smart use of tools.

Your career isn't threatened by AI. It's threatened by standing still.

Keep moving forward.

About the Series

'**The Glacier Series on *Asking AI*** is a bold, multi-volume exploration of questions about AI that will define humanity's future. These are questions posed to artificial intelligence, where the AI's response quietly guides the conversation. At the center of this series is not just the evolution of AI but the transformation of humanity itself.

The series is built on a foundational premise—that dialogue with machines, with ourselves and with the systems we inhabit is the most powerful tool we have for navigating uncertainty. Each book presents structured inquiries that raise pressing, often uncomfortable questions. Should AI ever govern? Can a machine inspire? What happens to learning when information is no longer scarce?

Rather than chase technical explanations or speculative extremes, the series keeps its gaze on the human interior—on identity, trust, purpose and the moral frameworks that underlie progress. Each book covers a different theme and collectively they paint a picture of a changing humanitarian landscape.

The Creative Process Behind the Series

The Glacier Series was born from a process of curated questioning. Drawing from thousands of structured interview questions with AI's ChatGPT, author David Glacier pursued a methodical yet deeply personal approach to shaping the series. Each question is treated not as a prompt for a single answer but as an aperture for insight.

Every book in the series emerged through iterative conversations between a human and a machine, crossing disciplines and incorporating the author's own editing of each response. The result is a body of work that resists dogma and instead welcomes ambiguity, always returning to the core human need to ask, to understand and to belong.

The Glacier Series on Asking AI is not a roadmap but a compass. It does not dictate a destination; instead, it reminds readers why the journey matters.

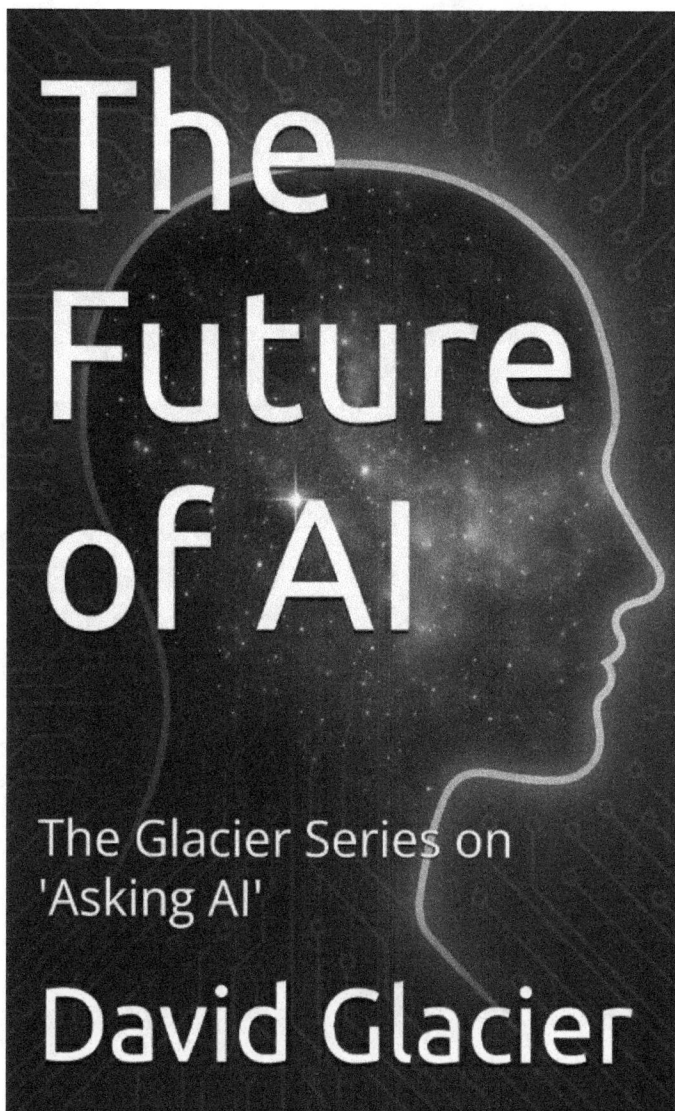

The Future of AI

The Glacier Series on 'Asking AI'

David Glacier

An Introduction to AI

The Glacier Series on 'Asking AI'

David Glacier

AI and Creativity

The Glacier Series on 'Asking AI'

David Glacier

AI and the Human Identity

The Glacier Series on 'Asking AI'

David Glacier

AI and Education

The Glacier series on 'Asking AI'

David Glacier

AI and Keeping Your Job

The Glacier series on 'Asking AI'

David Glacier

NOTES

www.ingramcontent.com/pod-product-compliance
Lightning Source LLC
Chambersburg PA
CBHW070943210326
41520CB00021B/7033